LEARN ABOUT ROBOTICS

Written by De-ann Black

TOP THAT! Kids™

Published by Top That! Publishing Inc.
25031 W. Avenue Stanford, Suite #60, Valencia, CA 91355
www.topthatpublishing.com
Copyright © 2005 Top That! Publishing plc
Top That! Kids is a trademark of Top That! Publishing plc
All rights reserved
0 2 4 6 8 9 7 5 3 1
Printed and bound in China

A HISTORY OF ROBOTS

Robots have been around for about 60 years, so they're not that old, but the idea of creating a robot goes back a long time in history. Ancient Greek legends spoke of maidens made of gold who were mechanical servants built by Hephaistos, the Greek god of metalsmiths.

THE FIRST PLANS

The first plans for a mechanical person were drawn in 1496 by Leonardo da Vinci. Amazingly, his drawings have been used by NASA to design futuristic robots because the artist's knowledge of the workings of the human body are some of the best ever drawn.

The Cyber Laws

1. A robot may not injure a human being, or, through inaction, allow a human being to come to harm;

2. A robot must obey orders given to it by human beings, except where such orders would conflict with the First Law; and

3. A robot must protect its own existence as long as such protection does not conflict with the First or Second Law.

CYBER LAWS

The word "robotics" was invented by Isaac Asimov in 1942. He also created the three laws of robots. He added a fourth law after the other three were written, stating that a robot may not injure humanity or, through inaction, allow humanity to come to harm.

Did You Know?

The word "robot" was first used in 1920 by the Czech playwright Karel Capek. It derives from the Czech word "robota" meaning forced labor, or servant.

ROBOTS FROM SCIENCE FICTION

Robots, such as Robbie the Robot (right), and the robot Maria from the 1927 film *Metropolis* (below), have become very popular through science fiction.

Maria the robot in the film Metropolis.

Robbie the Robot.

THE FIRST REAL ROBOTS

In the 1940s-1960s, the replacement of valves with transistors and integrated circuits, reliable electronics and the arrival of the computer industry, more or less, brought robots to life.

Did You Know?

The first working robot in the United Kingdom was made in 1928. Designed by Captain Rickards and A H Renfell, it was an electromechanical robot with an electric motor, electromagnets, pulleys, and wheels.

ELEKTRO & SPARKO

Two of the first famous robots were Elektro and his dog, Sparko. Built by Westinghouse Electric Corporation, they were shown at the World's Fair in New York in 1939. Elektro was a mechanical metal man that could dance and count to ten. Sparko the robot dog could walk, stand on its hind legs and bark.

Elektro and Sparko.

TURTLE POWER

In the 1940s, W Grey Walter developed turtle-like, mobile robotic vehicles called Machina Speculatrix. Two of these were named Elmer and Elsie (ELectro-MEchanical Robots, Light-Sensitive). His robots were special because they combined electronics and biology to give lifelike behavior—and were an early form of what we now call "artificial life."

Machina Speculatrix.

THE UNIMATE

In 1956, two men, George Devol and Joseph Engelberger, met and decided to start the world's first robot company, called Unimation. Their first robot was the Unimate. From this design the first commercial industry robot was made in 1959. It worked in a die-casting factory in America lifting hot pieces of metal.

Did You Know?
Robotics is the technology dealing with the design, construction and use of robots.

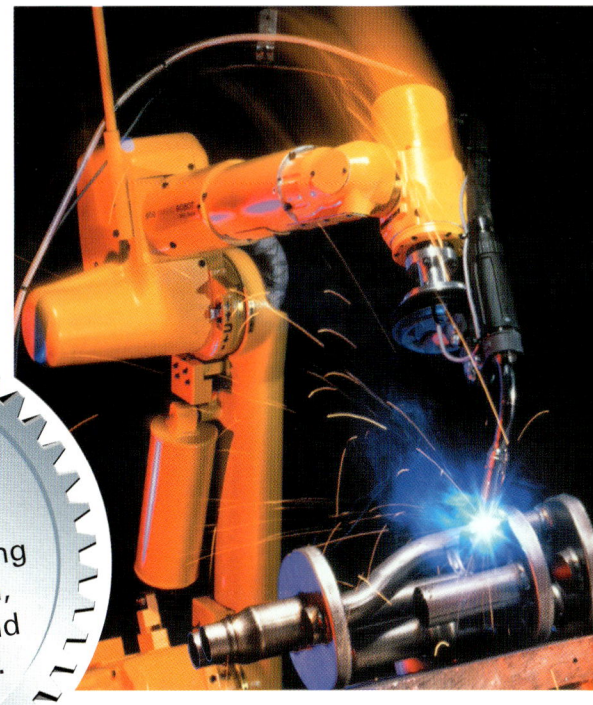

A robot welds a component in a factory.

FAMOUS ROBOTS

Robots have always caught the imagination and have featured in some of the most successful films and books of all time.

STAR WARS

C3PO and R2D2 in Star Wars.

Star Wars, one of the most popular films of all time, features the robots R2D2 and C3P0. Unlike many robots on film, these androids are good, not evil. They help the film's hero, Luke Skywalker, in his battles against Darth Vader.

BLADE RUNNER

In this cult classic, Harrison Ford stars as a man charged with hunting down artificially created humans who have hijacked a space ship.

ROBOCOP

Set in Detroit, USA, in the future, police officer Murphy, who is killed in the line of duty, is volunteered to be the test subject for some new cyborg technology. Robocop is then born and put back into the police force as a "super" cop. As Robocop discovers his past, he uncovers a murder conspiracy at the highest level of police management.

THE TERMINATOR

In this film a human-looking robot, played by Arnold Schwarzenegger, is sent from the future to kill Sarah Connor so that her son will not be born. The son is destined to lead the humans in a war against robots but stopping his birth will make this impossible.

The Terminator.

ARTIFICIAL INTELLIGENCE: AI

Steven Spielberg directed this film which stars Haley Joel Osment as David, the first robot to have feelings. When his mother rejects David in favor of her human child he struggles to regain her love.

WESTWORLD

This classic 1970s' sci-fi film tells the story of a futuristic amusement park where robots are employed to play whatever roles the customers want. When they are asked to perform a wild west adventure, however, one of the robots begins to behave independently and starts shooting at the customers.

BICENTENNIAL MAN

Bicentennial Man began life as a short story by Isaac Asimov before being made into a film. It tells the tale of a robot's 200-year journey to become human. At first, just a domestic robot intended to perform household chores, Bicentennial Man gradually gains human emotions.

Bicentennial Man.

SHORT CIRCUIT

This comedy film tells the story of an experimental robot called Number 5. After Number 5 is electrocuted, it develops self-awareness and a fear of being re-programmed. It therefore tries to escape its owners.

Number 5 from the film Short Circuit.

WHAT IS A ROBOT?

Many machines are programmed to do things, but most are clueless about their surroundings and aren't able to do physical tasks (such as moving objects).

ROBOT QUALIFICATIONS

For a machine to qualify as a robot, it must be able to do two things:

1. Be aware of its surroundings
2. Be able to do physical tasks

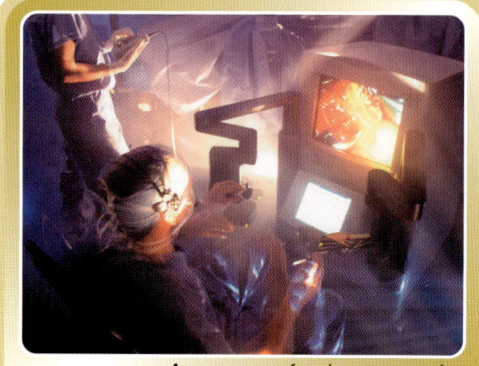

A surgeon performing an operation by remote robotics.

That's really what makes a robot a robot! No matter how hi-tech some pieces of equipment are, they're just machines. Robots are a lot more than that. They respond to their environment and gather information from their surroundings. They can go to places too dangerous for humans and bring back valuable information. They can even perform surgery.

A robotic vacuum cleaner.

Take a look at these popular definitions of a robot:

1 A re-programmable, multi-function machine, a robot imitates the actions or appearance of a human or other life creature.

2 A robot is any machine that automatically does work on its own—when it has been programmed by humans.

3 Robots are machines that are able to do the same things as humans or animals —such as understanding their surroundings, moving objects, and planning actions.

4 A robot is an intelligent and obedient, but impersonal, machine.

UNIVERSAL ROBOTS

There are more robots throughout the world than ever! Faster and less expensive computer processors have made robots smarter and extended their skills. Scientists are currently working on methods to make robots move and think better—to make them "intelligent"— and create universal robots that can do just about anything a human can do.

An automated factory assembly line.

ROBOT JOBS

As technology advances to build better robots, they are being given more of the jobs that humans can't, or don't want to, do—from the dangerous jobs to the more boring ones.

JOB VACANCY
Robot wanted to work all hours for no wages. Must be reliable, intelligent, strong, and have a good memory.

Okay, so this isn't how it is, but the theory is similar. Over ninety percent of robots work in factories on assembly-line tasks.

Robots are extremely efficient as welders in factories.

Robots welding in a car factory.

They do everything from spray painting cars, to sorting chocolates into boxes. Industrial robots like these don't have individual names or personalities, nor do they look like humans. They are anonymous machines programmed to do repetitive tasks. It's true that the design of these robots is based on the

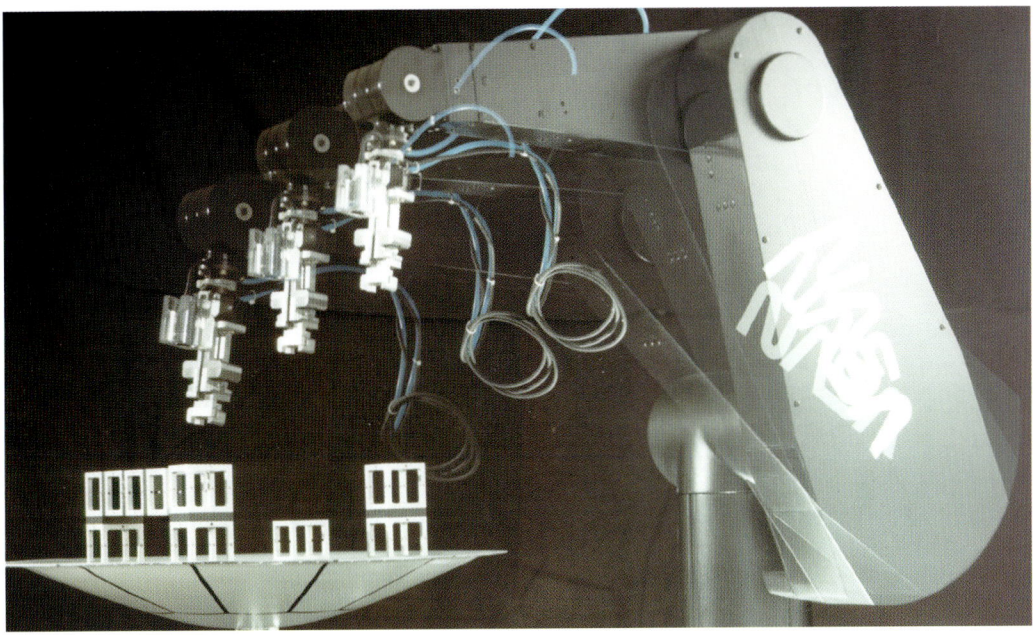

Programmable Universal Machine for Assembly: PUMA, is the most widely used industrial robot.

basic patterns of human biology (known as biomimetic locomotion), but the mass-market factory worker robots don't look like people. They're usually some kind of mechanical arm attached to a main machine.

EFFICIENT WORKERS

Robots are very efficient workers that don't get bored doing the same thing repeatedly—and they don't worry if their work is extremely dangerous!

In the not too distant future, robots will be monitoring pupils in school and helping to teach them.

Did You Know?

Biomimetic locomotion is the imitation of movement patterns in nature. A biomimetic robot is one of the latest inventions in robotics and it is believed that within the next two years, machines that can mimic human actions will be commercially available. They may even be able to help milk cows.

DANGEROUS WORK

Wow—robots do some of the most dangerous and exciting jobs!

HEAT HAZARD

Robots don't worry about walking into a volcano—their bodies are made to withstand the intense heat of the burning lava and toxic fumes. They search live volcanoes for clues about future eruptions. These robots have a spider-like design so they can climb up and down the walls of volcanoes.

NASA's Dante II *was used to explore Mt. Spurr.*

Dante II, a six-legged robot, was programmed to explore the active volcano of Mount Spurr, Alaska.

A bomb disposal robot.

DAREDEVILS

Bomb disposal work is something robots excel at. They are sent into buildings to search for bomb—and are able to defuse them once they find them. Brave and clever! Many have cameras mounted on them so that humans can watch what they're up to from a safe distance.

CYBER SPIES

Being a spy is a risky business, but robots are good at it. Venturing into enemy territory, seeking information, taking photographs, and then returning with the data is all part of being a robot spy. Their memories can store a vast amount of information, and as most of these robots are small, they are ideal for secret missions.

A robot-piloted plane.

HEAVY METAL

Powerful robotic arms can lift heavy objects easily, especially during emergency rescues. They can tear through metal and very often save the day!

Robot helicopters can fly close to danger to survey the scene.

DANGEROUS WORK

TOXIC CHEMICALS

Chemical substances that are toxic and harmful to humans often need to be handled—and what better to do it than a robot? Robots can go into infected areas and clean up the waste, or can be sent to investigate how poisonous some chemicals are.

SCIENTISTS

Robots in science labs are used quite often to test substances and handle dangerous materials that would be harmful to humans. The Waterblast robot (below) removes thermal protection materials and coatings from spaceflight hardware.

The Waterblast robot.

BARKING BOTS

Robot guard dogs are already here. The robotic pooches have a fierce-looking appearance and can snarl, growl and bark at intruders—as well as being able to alert the police!

A Banryu home security guard.

FIREFIGHTERS

Due to their strength and ability to survive extreme heat and smoke, robots of the future would make ideal firefighters. Small robots have been designed to protect properties against fire and intruders. They are programmed to know the layout of a property and on sensing a fire or break in security will alert the necessary authorities or owners of the house. In the future, robots will help to control fires before firefighters arrive at the scene.

SECURITY AGENTS

A new robotic security guard is being built. It follows human security agents (such as those inside a bank) and can carry money safely from one part of a building to another. It has various defence weapons which include sound and lamp menaces, electric shock capability, and a smoke shield device.

A demonstration of the Secom Cash Collection Delivery robot.

SARGE.

MILITARY ACTION

SARGE (Surveillance and Reconnaissance Ground Equipment) is a military robot. Developed for the US Marines, SARGE is sent into the field first. It helps the soldiers to decide what their future needs on the battlefield will be, so minimizing their personal risk.

EXPLORING EXTREMES

Robots are ideal for missions to extreme regions of the world because they are able to withstand icy conditions and dangerous terrain.

ICE ANDROIDS

A specially designed robot called *Nomad* explored the frozen Antarctic in search of meteorites. *Nomad* was an autonomous (self-operating), four-wheeled robot equipped with advanced controls and sophisticated sensors. It was the first robot to explore this extreme polar region and used a camera eye to search for and identify rocks. *Nomad* used a metal detector to identify iron in the rocks, this being a key metal in meteorites. A laser rangefinder helped it to navigate its surroundings.

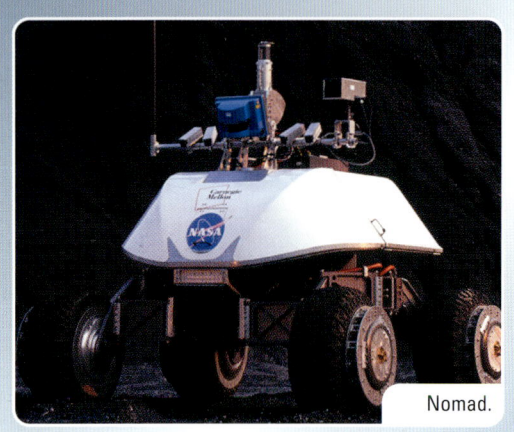

Nomad.

The Mars Polar lander.

SOLAR ROBOT

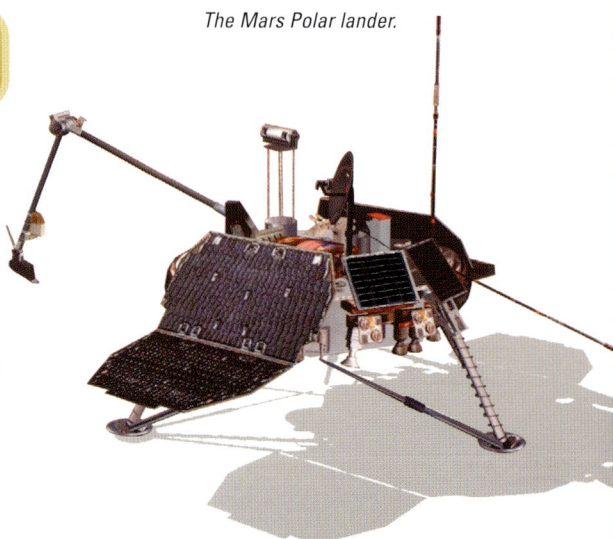

A solar-powered robot that follows the Sun was sent to explore the Arctic in the continuous sunlight of an Arctic summer. The robot was called *Hyperion* (named after the Titan in Greek mythology who was the father of the Sun, the Moon, and the dawn). *Hyperion* used solar power to navigate (called sun-synchronous navigation). It captured enough sunlight to power itself while exploring the Arctic. *Hyperion* moved as the Sun circled the sky.

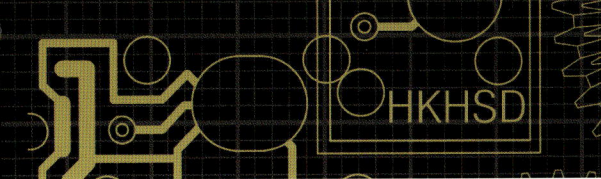

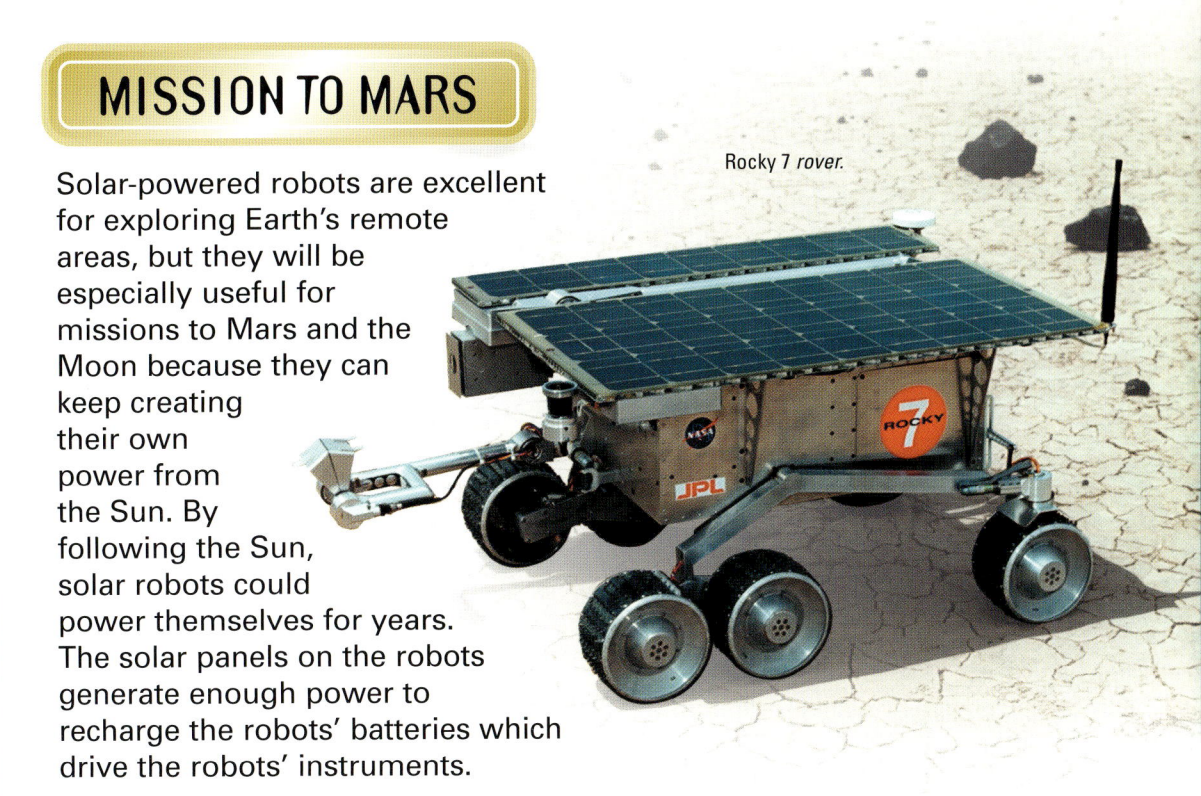

MISSION TO MARS

Solar-powered robots are excellent for exploring Earth's remote areas, but they will be especially useful for missions to Mars and the Moon because they can keep creating their own power from the Sun. By following the Sun, solar robots could power themselves for years. The solar panels on the robots generate enough power to recharge the robots' batteries which drive the robots' instruments.

Rocky 7 rover.

UNDERWATER ROBOTS

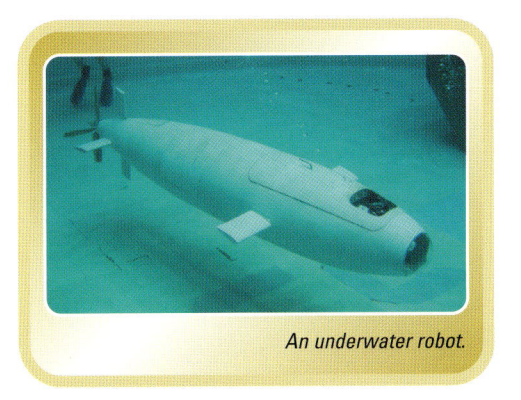

Deep-sea robots are a new development in oceanography. Vast areas of the world's oceans have never been explored, but now they can be with the help of underwater robots. Some of these robots look like sea creatures, such as lobsters, while others resemble mini submarines.

An underwater robot.

EXPLORING EXTREMES

TITANIC

An underwater robot called *JJ* (*Jason Junior*) explored the wreck of the ship *Titanic* that sank in the Atlantic in 1912. The *Titanic* had been lying at the bottom of the sea for 74 years before *JJ* was sent down in 1986 to a depth of 12,470 ft to explore it. The robot was an ROV (remote operated vehicle).

The Slocum seaglider, an AUV.

The Slocum glider being adjusted.

AUVs

New technology has led to the development of underwater robots called autonomous underwater vehicles (AUVs). They use clever software to navigate by themselves using onboard computers. They usually look like small submarines and are equipped with the latest technology to search the depths of our oceans. A few are oddly designed, like sea creatures, and walk on numerous legs along the bottom of the sea.

AUTOSUB ROBOT

A UK robot known as Autosub is used to explore beneath the icy water of the Antarctic. Under the freezing glaciers, the robot collects information from this extreme location. The robot sub carries its own power supply (batteries), and uses its sensors to collect data from the ocean surface and the seabed.

WINGED ROBOTS

These robots don't fly, despite their name. They dive to great depths in the ocean. The wings help them glide through the water, diving down to the bottom of the sea. Some of these robots were sent into the waters of the Gulf of Mexico to study red tides (mysterious masses of red toxic plankton that kill fish and poison seafood). Winged robots are AUVs that beam their data to researchers via satellite.

ENTERTAINING ROBOTS

Robots are a lot of fun! They make great pets, compete in fighting competitions—and dance! It's not just the toy market that has been developing robotic gizmos and gadgets—robots have reached a competitive level where they compete in world championship events! Not only are these competitions exciting, they also help invent new robotic technology.

ROBOT SPORTS

More robots than ever are competing at sporting events, such as the Robot Football World Championships, where small robots play football—and there's a category for biped (two-legged) humanoid robots to dribble the ball down the pitch or stand

Robotic football.

in front of the goal and take penalty kicks! Other sporting contests include gladiator events, obstacle courses, and even robot marathons!

Humanoid robots playing football.

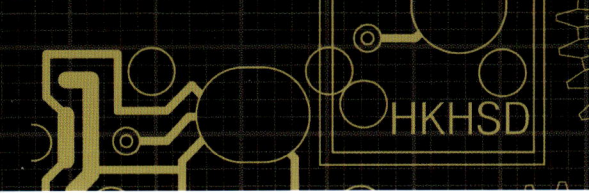

KUNG FUSED

Robots pack quite a punch! They fight each other inside boxing rings and also do martial arts! Fighting robots are becoming very popular and large crowds are drawn to these knockout events.

DANCING DROIDS

Dancing robots show the extent of the skills these humanoids can achieve. DJ droids are being experimented with. A robot DJ played music at a nightclub (along with a real DJ). Many of the clubbers thought the droid was a real DJ star.

DOGGIE DROID

Robotic dogs now make quite popular pets. Sony's AIBO (eye-bo) Entertainment Robot 220 has sensors that make it react like a real pet dog.

Sony's robotic dog.

ROBOT TROLLEY

In Yo! Sushi, a Japanese restaurant, there is a robot waiter. While it can't take your order, it will bring your drinks to the table. It has sensors to prevent it bumping into things and can detect people if they get in its way.

Paro, the seal robot.

SEAL ROBOT

Paro, the seal robot, is taken to hospitals to play with young patients to calm them. This is known as robot-assisted therapy (RAT).

ANDROIDS AND HUMANOIDS

An android is an anthropomorphic robot (which means it looks like a human). Many android developers prefer to call them humanoids, but they're really both the same thing.

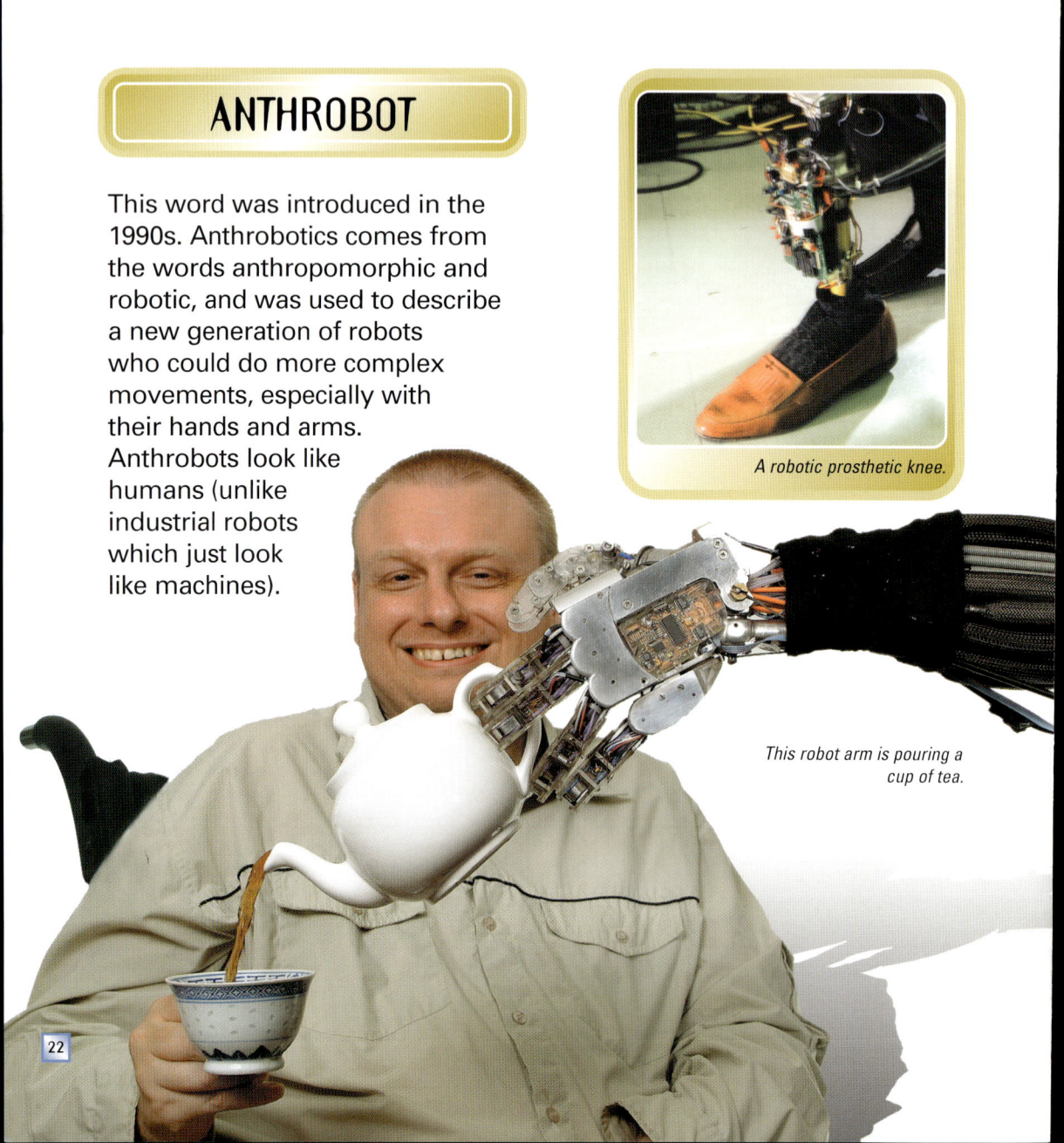

ANTHROBOT

This word was introduced in the 1990s. Anthrobotics comes from the words anthropomorphic and robotic, and was used to describe a new generation of robots who could do more complex movements, especially with their hands and arms. Anthrobots look like humans (unlike industrial robots which just look like machines).

A robotic prosthetic knee.

This robot arm is pouring a cup of tea.

PROGRAMMING

Programming involves making instructions and tasks for the robot. Sometimes only a few instructions are used, but numerous tasks can be created to run throughout the program. There are lots of programming languages, most of them available to be installed into a computer and then downloaded into specific robots.

Robots are programmed to follow instructions.

BINARY CODE

Most languages are based on mathematical concepts (such as the binary system), using numbers to equate to certain commands. Robots work via a computer link or, if they're really hi-tech, autonomously (on their own, using the program that is installed into their circuits). Commercial robots, especially toys, are often pre-programmed so the customer doesn't need to program them, or can upgrade and re-program them once the robots have learned everything they can achieve at a certain level. Using computer language, robots can be programmed to respond to simple commands. Complex programs are based on artificial intelligence.

Elektra is a pre-programmed movable robot.

AI—ARTIFICIAL INTELLIGENCE

Artificial intelligence is the science of making intelligent machines (especially computer programs). One of the main aims of AI is to create computer programs that have human-level intelligence so that they can solve problems and achieve goals as well as humans. These programs will build robots that can think on a level equal to humans.

ARTIFICIAL SYSTEMS

Basically, AI is natural information processing in an artificial system. It takes the basic abilities of the human brain and puts that intelligence capability into a machine.

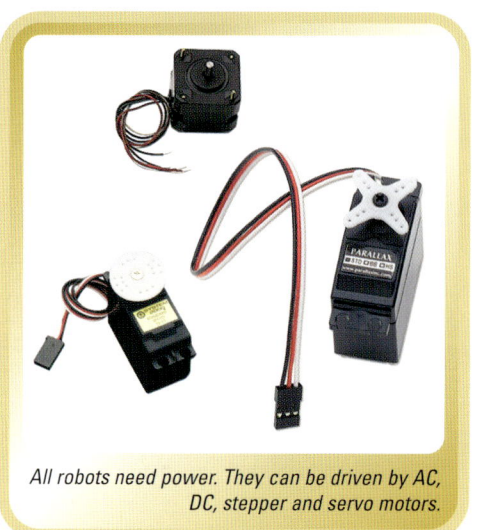

Robots are controlled by a system of computer controls and switches.

All robots need power. They can be driven by AC, DC, stepper and servo motors.

Most AI programs use rule-based logic. This is the type of logic used by computers. Binary data is stored and accessed using a set of pre-programmed rules. Robotic brains are very often rule-based. They use a single chip that functions as a computer. This is called a microcomputer. Rule-based computer programs contain vast amounts of information.

COG

Cog.

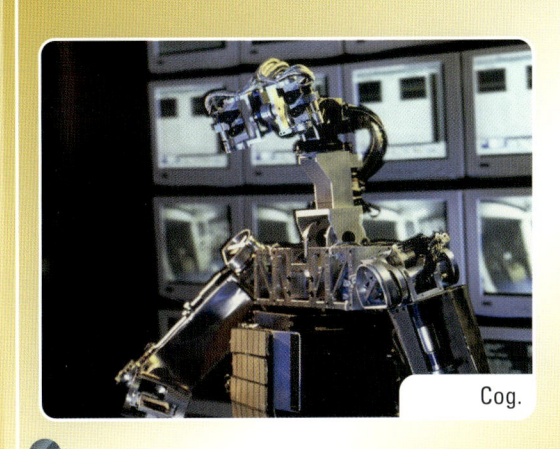

Cog (short for cognitive), is an android robot developed as part of artificial intelligence research. *Cog* can co-ordinate its hearing and visual systems to pinpoint a noise source. The visual system can guide hand movements. *Cog* is used to study how humans learn through interaction with people.

NEURAL NETWORKS

Another form of AI is called "neural networks"—where robots try to mimic the human brain. These brain boxes are very good at making decisions rather as we do. Sometimes there are no definite answers, only probable ones to questions such as "Will you enjoy lunch?" and "Will the weather be warm?," and "Will my favorite team win the game?." A neural network understands this and gives a probable answer. This is often called "fuzzy logic"—a sort of grey area where various answers are logically possible.

Deep Blue, *a computer with similar abilities to an AI machine, was able to beat world champion Garry Kasparov at chess.*

MEMORY AND PROCESSING

Robots really need to have a good memory. They've got to store a vast amount of information and process it quickly and efficiently.

MEMORY CHIPS

New technology and less expensive computer processors and memory chips have enabled scientists and inventors to build better robots. The latest microchips can process a vast amount of data, and new chips are being produced every year, so the advances in computer technology and robotics are brilliant. More and more computer power means robots will one day be able to process information as we do. They will mimic us.

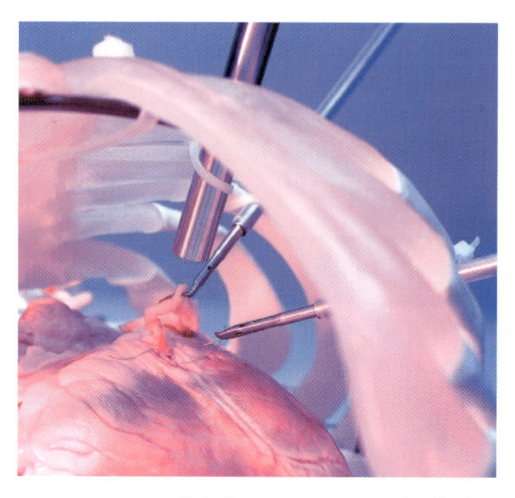

Robotic surgery an example of robots mimicking humans.

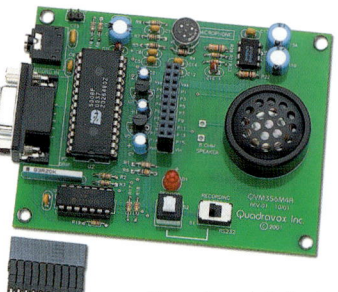

At the moment, an average computer has 1000 MIPS of power. (MIPS stands for millions of instructions per second). 1000 MIPS is roughly the brain power of an insect. However, within the next 30 years, scientists believe that robots will achieve 100,000,000 MIPS—human-level intelligence.

Stamp boards tell robots what to do.

SENSOR CIRCUITRY

Robots need sensors to obtain information about their surroundings. Basically, a sensor "senses" things around it and makes an electric signal. This gives the robot the information it needs to move around and do various tasks. Robot sensors are designed to mimic human senses.

LIGHT SENSORS

Robotic light sensors are used for basic navigation. Some robots' sensors "see" light and are designed to have various responses to it. Other robots use ultrasonic sound (as bats do) to "see." The robots send out sound waves (which humans can't hear), and detect echoes. They measure the time delay (of sending the sound to hearing the echo) to work out the distance of objects.

Robotic vision is a complex system. It involves light sensors and a camera eye. Images are processed by a computer program. To create this type of vision, large amounts of computer memory are needed.

The K9 rover, a robot capable of navigation.

MEMORY AND PROCESSING

TOUCH

Feelers, contact switches, and bump sensors are all different sorts of touch sensors. They let robots know when they've bumped into something. Some touch sensors are made from piezoelectric crystals (such as quartz) that can detect vibration, impact, and heat. Piezoelectric crystals create an electric field when "stressed." Piezoelectric comes from the Greek word "piezein" meaning "squeeze," and from the electricity created by the crystals when under pressure.

The iBOTZ Soundtracker robot reacts to sound impulses and objects in its path. It will reverse away from the sound or obstruction, then move forward.

POSITION SENSORS

These are useful for industrial robots working in factories that need to remember all the positions their "arms" have to be in at certain points of the assembly line. The sensors actually "remember" where they are supposed to go.

The Antoid walks on six legs and uses its infrared eye to detect and avoid objects in its path.

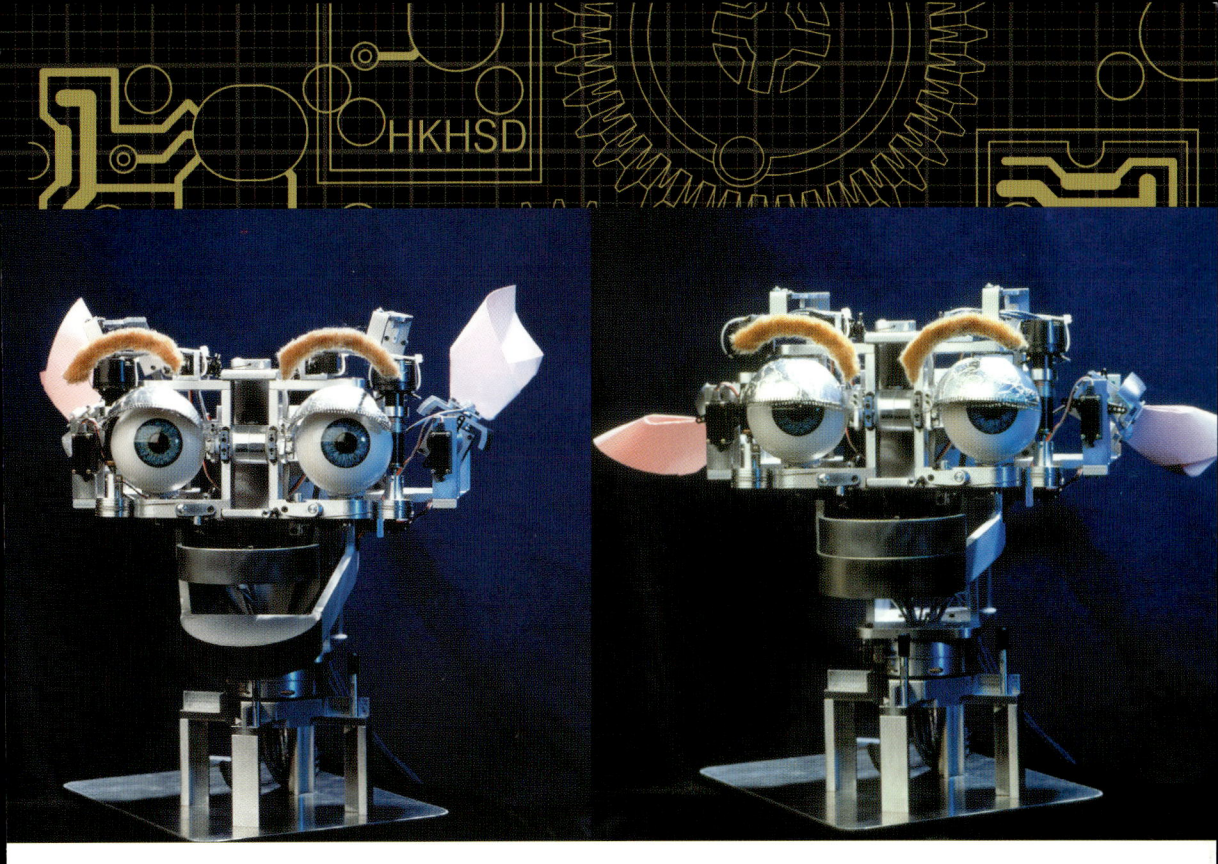

Kismet *the robot picks up human expressions to develop its own "personality."*

Cyberguard can detect smells.

OTHER SENSES

Human senses can be very difficult to replicate in robots because vision, touch, hearing, smell, and taste are extremely subjective. For instance, something that feels cold to one person may feel warm to another. Taste is the least developed robot sense.

Robot technology is advancing all the time and, currently, robots are particularly good at detecting gases (especially those that are poisonous to humans) and hidden explosives.

MOTION AND MOTORS

One of the main things that makes a robot different from a computer is that it can move about. "Actuator" is the word that's used to describe a mechanical device that produces motion. One robot can have numerous actuators to do various tasks.

The Dyson DC06 robotic vacuum cleaner.

ACTUATORS

An electric motor is a type of actuator. It produces motion from electricity using the electromagnetic effect. Electricity moves through a coil of wire that is near a magnet and this force pushes on the coil. Most electric motors have a high speed and small turning power. However, most robots need low speed and plenty of power, so special engines have to be made and adjusted to suit the robots.

SOLENOIDS

Some electric motors produce turning motion, but some don't. That's where solenoids come in—they are electric motors that produce an in-and-out motion (linear motion). Solenoids are used in switches to turn things off and on—and are often part of robotic motion.

SERVO MOTOR

One of the hardest motions for a robot to do is walk. Special stepper motors turn in "steps" and this makes them perfect for small, repeated movements. Servo motors are popular for controlling positioning. Remote-controlled cars often have their steering controlled by a servo motor.

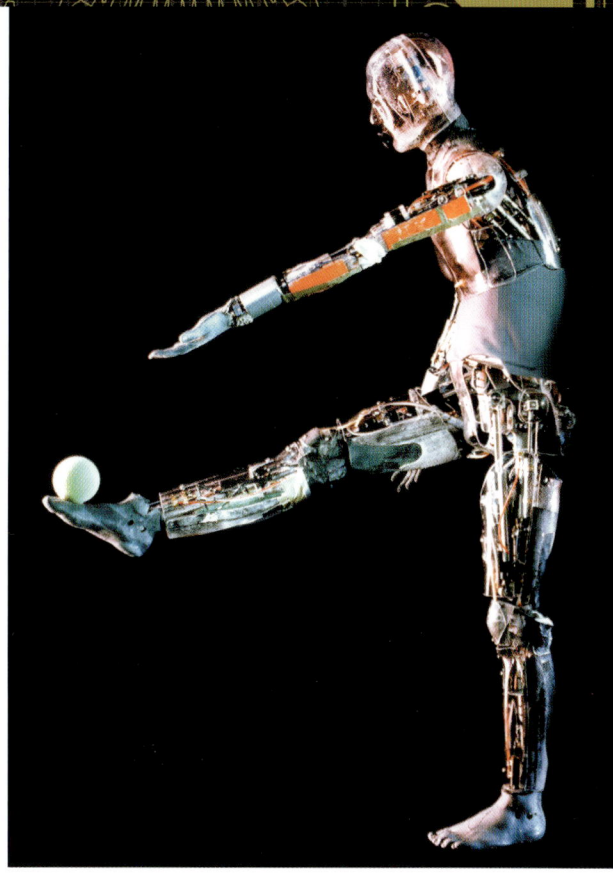

The movable sections of robots are usually made of either plastic or metal.

HYDRAULIC & PNEUMATIC

Hydraulic actuators use oil to move and pneumatic ones use gas. There are many types of actuators used to make robots move as humans.

Androids use actuators as "muscles" to move.

ROBOT BODY PARTS

ALL ROBOTS ARE MADE UP OF THREE THINGS:
1. BODY
2. CONTROLS
3. BEHAVIOR

The controls and behavior are determined by the sort of programming, processing, and sensors the robot has. Now let's look at the body parts.

Okay, so there are lots of body types—human, animal, monster, and machine. First, let's study some of the main body parts of a robotic car because many robots are based on a chassis and wheels.

NASA's Mars 2003 rover.

These make up the platform that holds the motor and program systems and allows the robot to move around on the wheels.

BODY

The chassis is the main body part (platform). Wheels are attached to the chassis and allow varying ranges of movement backward and forward and turning left and right. The wheels are usually designed to provide good traction (grip) on different types of surface. Custom-built body parts are then added to the central chassis to create the robotic car. A well-structured chassis and wheels are a priority for vehicles such as NASA's Mars rover that has to trundle across rough terrain.

Nanorover.

Dalek robots, from the TV show Dr Who, were monster warrior robots.

MONSTERS

We usually think of robots as having a human appearance. Robots of the past have tended to be rather odd-looking metal androids. Robots of the future will be very lifelike. Already some realistic robotic heads with moving eyes have been designed. The faces can make different expressions and look so real that they're almost creepy! Some heads are made to resemble weird monsters, dinosaurs, and reptiles!

This robotic fish houses electronics that help it move.

HOUSING

A robot is full of sensitive electronics which need to be protected. Fortunately, unlike a human, a robot's body does not require a heart, lungs, or kidneys. This means that the robot's body can be used to house and protect the vital electronics.

ROBOT BODY PARTS

A robotic planetary exploration vehicle prototype that moves on wheels.

ARMS & HANDS

A robotic hand that resembles that of a human.

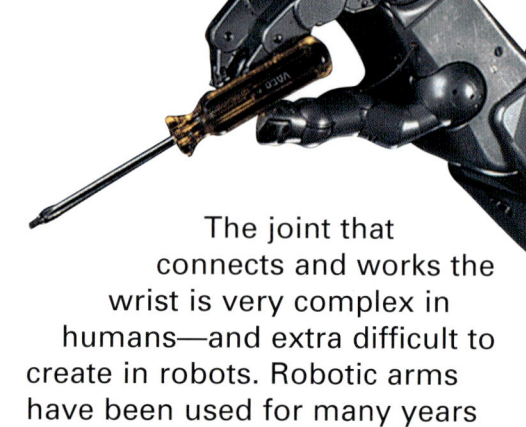

The joint that connects and works the wrist is very complex in humans—and extra difficult to create in robots. Robotic arms have been used for many years for industrial work, but many of these are limited in what they can do. Scientists hope to be able to make arms and hands that have the same range of movements as humans. The most sophisticated robot hands, such as those of NASA's Robonaut, are able to grasp and manipulate all sorts of objects. In this way, they replicate the human hand.

LEGS & FEET

Making a robot's legs and feet is very difficult. The robot has to be able to balance properly on them when standing and walking. Walking is one of the hardest movements to achieve. Recently, inventors have designed a robot that can get up by itself from a sitting position on the ground. No mean feat!

Bomb disposal robots pass over obstacles using "caterpillar tracks."

34

ANIMAL PARTS

Robotic pets are popular toys, but the animal world is being used as inspiration to build robots that can dive to the depths of the ocean, climb up walls, growl at intruders and even fly. Animals, birds and insects have great abilities, and these are being reproduced in robots.

The body parts of a beetle have enormous strength, speed and agility so this structure has been copied to make mine-seeking robots that can scuttle into caves. Spider-like robots can climb up walls, and flying insects can soar on robotic wings! Small artificial wings flap like real fly wings and generate lift.

A jellyfish robot!

A spider-bot prototype.

HEAD

As with a human, a robot's seeing and hearing devices are found on the head. The difference is that the robot's head can turn 360° independently.

BRAIN

All robots have a computer for a brain. The robot can only act as commanded by the computer. If the computer has been programmed only to give the robot one command, then that will be the only order the robot can follow.

CYBERNETICS

Cybernetics is the study of biological and artificial control systems. Scientists compare the ways in which humans and machines work. The aim is to allow humans to perform tasks using their own nervous systems and computer transmission. For example, a microchip could be implanted in the human body that would send and receive information via the nervous system and a computer!

BLUEPRINT

Scientists are studying the automatic communication and control system in the human body—and in mechanical electronic systems (such as a computer). By studying human nervous and biological systems, they aim to discover a sort of "blueprint" of human nature. The blueprint would then be programmed into robots.

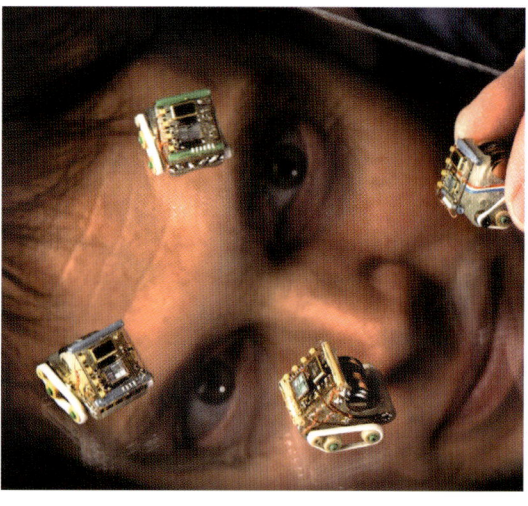

Mini robots are currently being researched.

STEERSMAN

Norbert Wiener wrote a book about cybernetics in 1948. He was the first to use the name cybernetics, which he took from the Greek word "kybernetes," meaning "steersman."

Did You Know?
Cyborg means cybernetic organism. Natural and artificial systems are combined to create a cyborg.

Robots can have a body structure similar to a human's.

CYBORG

British scientists are said to have implanted cybernetic technology into the arm of a man, enabling his nervous system to be linked to a computer. Some consider him to be the world's first cyborg—part human, part machine. It is hoped this type of technology will prove useful to medical science in the future.

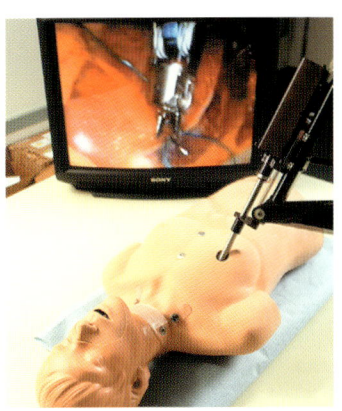

A robot performing an operation.

EXCITING EXPERIMENTS

ROBOT BLOOD
Make your own robot blood!

You will need...
- pieces of rust (flakes of iron) or powdered iron filings
- vegetable oil
- a small plastic or glass container
- a magnet

ADULT SUPERVISION REQUIRED!
Ask an adult to supervise when you are doing these experiments. Take care when using and handling iron. Use a plastic spoon to handle the iron and always wash your hands afterwards if you touch the rust.

METHOD

1. Pour some vegetable oil into the container (enough to cover the bottom of the container).

2. Mix some pieces of rust (a few flakes is ideal) into the oil.

3. Hold a magnet near the mixture and see how the rust joins up in a line and stiffens in the oil. If you move the magnet away, the rust will relax again.

Did You Know?

On the International Space Station, astronauts are experimenting with "robot blood." They call it magnetorheological fluids (MR fluids). The gooey fluid they use is magnetized. When it is exposed to an electromagnet, the fluid stiffens. This strange fluid may be used to flow in the veins of future robots, and be used to make the robots' joints move like humans.

The International Space Station.

EXCITING EXPERIMENTS

MAKE YOUR OWN ELECTROMAGNET

An electromagnet is the basis of an electric motor and is often used when powering robots. The motor uses magnets and magnetism to create motion. Inside an electric motor the forces created by a magnet "attracting" and "repelling" things cause the motor to rotate (move).

You will need...

- a large metal household nail
- a piece of metal wire
- sticky putty
- a small battery (ordinary AA household battery)
- adult supervision

Basically, by running an electric current through a wire, a magnetic field is created. Electromagnetism is used in lots of things including computers (disc drives and hard drives), motors and solenoids—many things used to create robots.

So, here's how to make your own electromagnet. Make sure you ask an adult to help you.

Electromagnets are used in the motors that drive these rescue robot buggies.

METHOD

1. Wrap the wire around the nail ten times. Leave enough wire at either end to connect it to the battery.

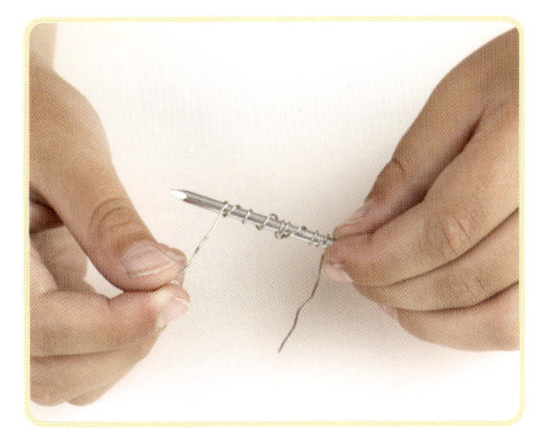

2. Connect each end of the wire to the top and bottom end (two terminals) of the battery. One is is positive (+) and the other is negative (−).

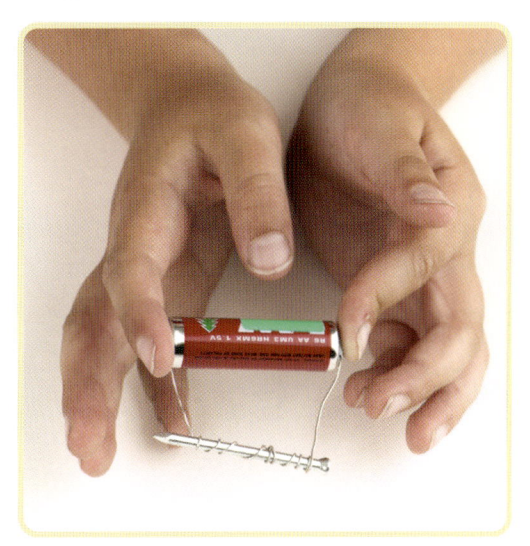

3. Congratulations! You've made an electromagnet! Test it by using it to pick up paper clips, staples and any small bits of steel or iron.

The paper clips are attracted only when electrons are flowing. When the power is turned off, the paper clips will fall off.

EXCITING EXPERIMENTS

ROBOT ARMS

Humans have seven degrees of freedom in each arm. This means that a human arm can make seven different types of movement. A robot arm needs six degrees of freedom (most jointed-arm robots have six, but some have 8-12). Each direction a joint can go is called a degree.

A robotic arm is a complex piece of technology. To understand how hard it is to build one of these, take a look at how your own arms work.

Your shoulder has three degrees, your arm has one, and your wrist has three. Try this test!

1st degree

SHOULDER PITCH—point your arm straight out in front of you. Move your shoulder up and down. The up and down movement of the shoulder is called pitch.

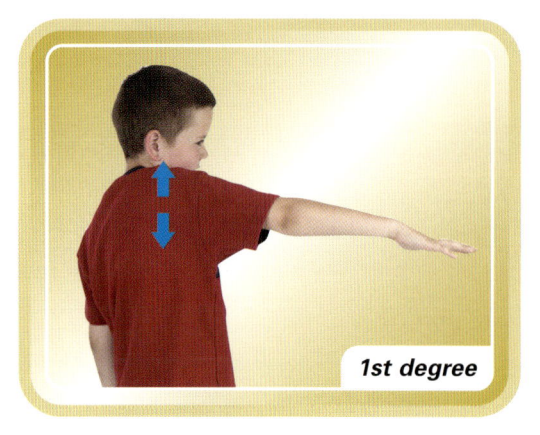

1st degree

2nd degree

ARM YAW—point your arm straight out in front of you. Move your arm from side to side. This is called yaw.

3rd degree

SHOULDER ROLL—point your arm straight out in front of you. Roll your shoulder joint.

42

4th degree

ELBOW PITCH—point your arm straight out in front. Hold your upper arm still and bend your elbow. Your elbow moves up and down. This is called elbow pitch.

4th degree

5th degree

WRIST PITCH—point your arm straight out in front. Keep your arm still and flex your wrist up and down.

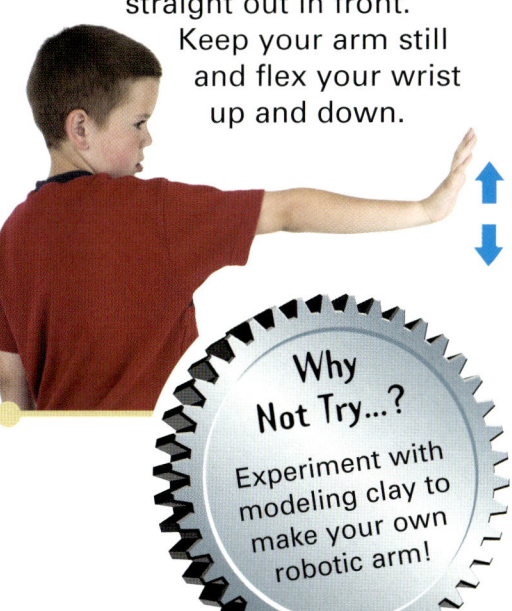

Why Not Try…?
Experiment with modeling clay to make your own robotic arm!

6th degree

WRIST YAW—as 5th degree, but move your wrist from side to side.

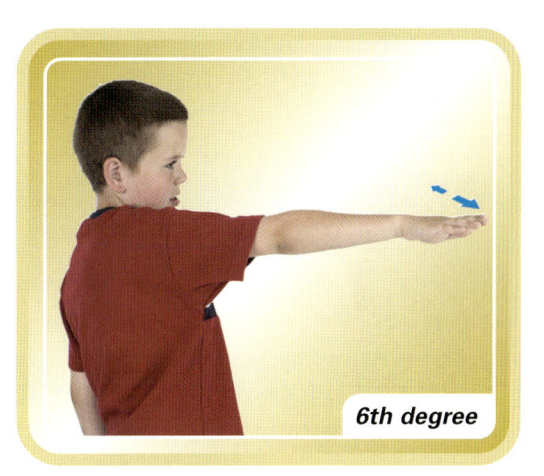

6th degree

7th degree

WRIST ROLL—as 5th degree, but rotate your wrist, as if you were drawing a circle in the air while keeping your arm still.

EXPLORING MARS

Europe's Mars Express, carrying the British-built Beagle 2 (a small spacecraft), blasted off from Baikonur Cosmodrome in Kazakhstan in June 2003. The European Space Agency's Mars Express mission aim was to discover whether there is, or was, life on Mars.

BEAGLE 2

The spacecraft was launched on top of a Russian Soyuz rocket. Within 92 minutes, it was injected into its interplanetary orbit. This was Europe's first mission to Mars.

Beagle 2 was set to look for evidence of past, or present, life (known as exobiology) on Mars. It was the first probe to make this its main mission aim and had the support of the British National Space Centre (BNSC).

ROBOT PAW

At the end of *Beagle 2*'s arm, was a PAW (position adjustable workbench) where various hi-tech instruments were kept. These included cameras and rock scrapers. A robot, known as the Mole, was designed to dig for soil samples. *Beagle 2*'s gas analysis package (GAP) could heat up rock and soil and analyse the gases created.

Professor Colin Pillinger and a Beagle 2 model.

All photographs of the Beagle 2 *on this spread ©* Beagle 2.

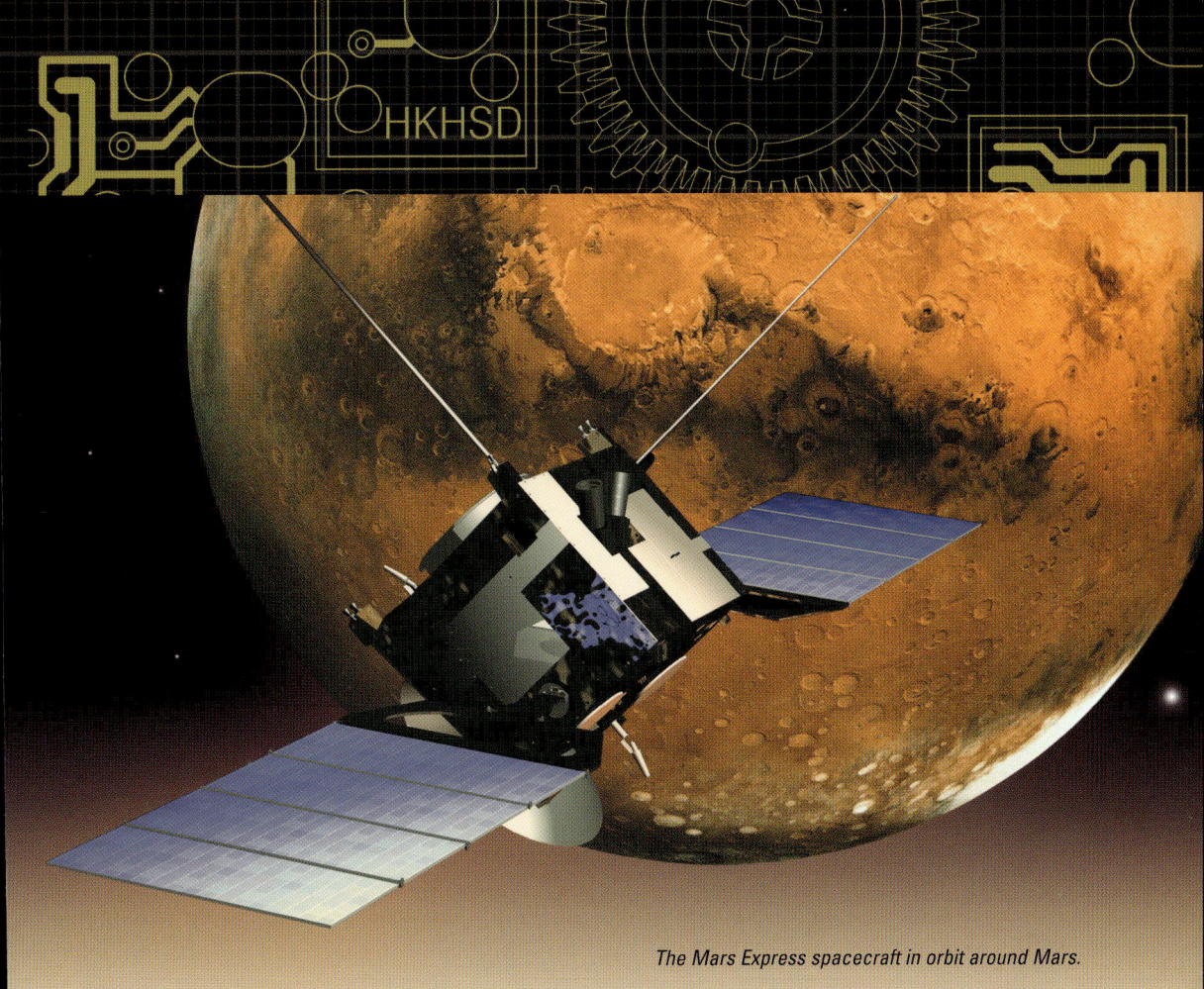

The Mars Express spacecraft in orbit around Mars.

Beagle 2 was ejected from the Mars Express orbiter and parachuted down to the surface of Mars. Meanwhile, the Mars Express orbiter used a near-polar orbit to observe the planet.

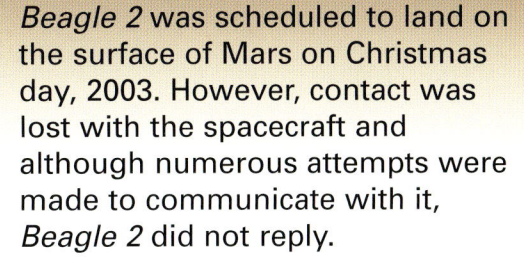

Beagle 2 was scheduled to land on the surface of Mars on Christmas day, 2003. However, contact was lost with the spacecraft and although numerous attempts were made to communicate with it, *Beagle 2* did not reply.

Beagle 2—*sent to look for life on Mars.*

Beagle 2.

FUTURISTIC ROBOTS

Robonaut is NASA's humanoid robot. The plan is to develop Robonaut to be an assistant to astronauts. NASA wants to build robots that can help humans work and explore space.

ROBONAUT

Working alongside humans, *Robonaut* will increase the ability of NASA to learn about the universe's ability to undertake operations too dangerous for humans is sure to improve our understanding of space.

DESIGN

Robonaut is already quite advanced. Dexterous manipulation (use of its hands/arms) is being developed in *Robonaut* so it can use its hands with better ability than a human wearing an astronaut's spacesuit.

Robonaut.

NASA scientists also aim to have it use its hands better than a human without a spacesuit too! It has 150 sensors in each arm, hands with four fingers and a thumb—and can even shake hands! The humanoid design (it's the size of an average astronaut) was created because NASA want the robot to be capable of spacewalks or Extravehicular Activity (EVA)—tasks not specifically designed for robots. It is being built to have excellent strength and endurance.

ROBOT'S VIEW

Inside the body is a CPU (central processing unit) which is part of the computerized controls. Using telepresence, a human operator controls the actions of the remotely controlled robot.

Telepresence uses virtual reality technology so that the teleoperator feels as if they are in the robot's workspace.

The teleoperator wears a display helmet that lets them view live video from the cameras on *Robonaut's* head (these are the robot's eyes). So they see what the robot sees!

The humanoid design of Robonaut *will enable it to spacewalk.*

Did You Know?

The humanoid has a computer brain and a rechargeable power source. The torso (main body) is made of an aluminum endoskeleton (internal skeleton or body framework) that is covered by a protective shell. *Robonaut* appears to have a remarkable future ahead!

FUTURISTIC ROBOTS

SPACE MECHANICS

It costs a lot of money to put a satellite into space. What happens when something malfunctions on the satellite? Sometimes the damage can be repaired via signals from Earth to the satellite, but often it ends up as a very expensive piece of space junk.

Robot mechanics could change all that. Robots could, in the future, be sent into space to go to the assistance of any satellite that needed a repair.

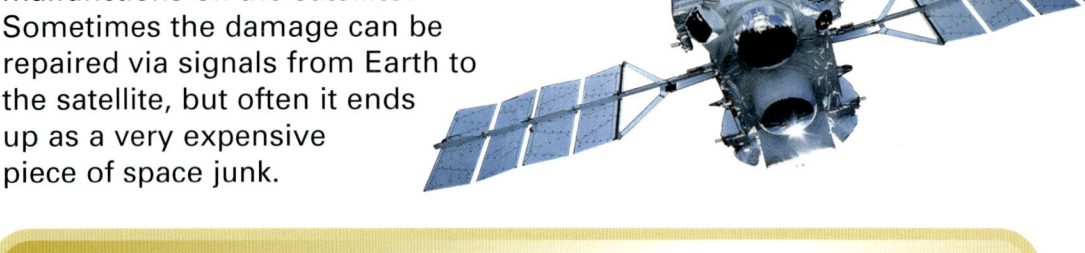

FUTURE FRIENDS

PaPeRo Robots

Robots of the future may be playing games with you at home, helping with your studies, and being your friend! Robotic toys are already commercially available and this type of cyber companion could become part of ordinary life.

Key: top - t; bottom - b; middle - m; left - l; right - r; Science Photo Library - SPL; Scandia National Laboratories - Courtesy of Scandia National Laboratories, Intelligents Systems and Robotics Center.

1: iBOTZ. 2: Bettmann/Corbis Sygma 3: (r) Bettmann/Corbis Sygma; (b) Snap/Rex features 4: Bettmann/Corbis Sygma 5: (t) TTAT; (b) David Parker,600 Group Franuc/SPL. 6-7: Allstar. 8: (t) NASA; (b) Peter Menzel/SPL. 9: Maximilan stock Ltd/SPL. 10: (t) Rex Features; (b) David Parker/SPL. 11: NASA. 12: (t) Labat/Lancean/Jerrican/SPL; (b) Hank Morgan/SPL. 13: (t) Rex Features; (b) Peter Menzel/SPL 14: (t) Sanyo Electric co./Ltd; (b) NASA. 15: (t) Masatoshi Okauchi/Rex Features; (b) Scandia National Laboratories. 16: (t) Peter Menzel/SPL; (b); NASA 17: NASA. 18: Webb Research. 19: Dave Doubilet/Webb Research. 20: The RoboCup Federation. 21: (m) Tony Kyriacou/Rex Features; (b) Sony Corporation. 22: (t) Peter Menzel/SPL; (b) Rex Features. 23: (t) Jerry Mason/SPL; (b) Volker Steger/SPL. 24: (t) Parallax Inc. 25: (t) Sam Ogden/SPL; (b) Pendzich/Rex Features. 26: (t) Rex Features; (b) Parallax Inc. 27: NASA. 28: iBOTZ. 29: (t) Sam Ogden/SPL; (b) Cybermotion. 30: Dyson. 31: (t) US Department of Energy/SPL; (b) Peter Menzel/SPL. 32: NASA. 33: (tl); NASA; (tr) Allstars, (b) Miyoko Oyashik/Corbis Sygma. 34: (t) NASA; (b) Volker Steger/SPL. 35: (t) Hashimoto Noboru/Corbis Sygma; (b) NASA. 36: Scandia National Laboratories. 37: (t) NASA; (b) Hank Morgan/SPL. 38: Top That! 39: (t) TopThat!; (b) NASA. 40: Scandia National Laboratories. 41-43: Top That! 44: All rights reserved Beagle 2 . 45: (t) ESA 2001, Media lab; (b) All rights reserved Beagle 2. 46: Peter Menzel/SPL. 47: (t) Rex Features. 48: (t) Photodisc; (m) courtesy of Nec Coporation 2002 .